MASKED HERO

MASKED HERO

How Wu Lien-teh Invented the Mask That Ended an Epidemic

Dr. Shan Woo Liu
and Kaili Liu Gormley

illustrated by
Lisa Wee

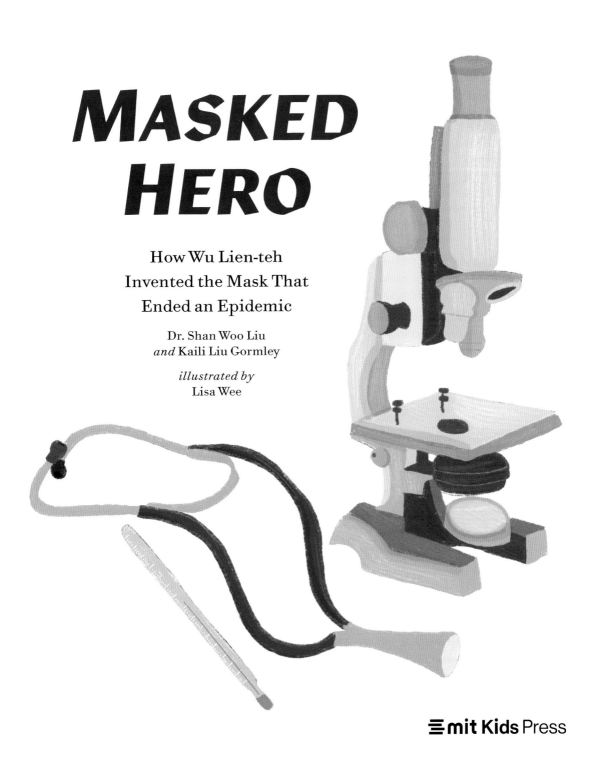

≡ mit Kids Press

WU LIEN-TEH grew up on a busy street in Malaysia, then a British colony called Malaya, in the late 1800s. On a typical day, the Chinese and Indian people who lived in his neighborhood mingled in the road as carriages and rickshaws wheeled past the shops selling cloth and fruit and brightly colored candies.

Yet the bustle outside was nothing compared to the laughter and shouting that filled the house where Lien-teh lived with his parents and ten brothers and sisters.

With the constant chatter, Lien-teh could hardly get any studying done. So he stayed up late every night, after the rest of his family had gone to sleep. His house had no electricity, so he studied by a lantern filled with coconut oil. He wanted to be a doctor when he grew up, and he needed good grades to do that.

His school, the Penang Free School, encouraged freedom of thought and belief, and Lien-teh was always thinking quickly and creatively. The school had no equipment for sports, so he and his classmates turned broken bookcases into cricket bats and writing slates into tennis rackets.

Lien-teh excelled in his classes and competed for a scholarship to attend college in England. To win, he needed top marks on the entrance exam. He took the test four times before finally nabbing the highest score.

Winning the scholarship was an honor, but his family fretted about sending him to school so far away. The year before, Lien-teh had suffered a bout of typhoid—a disease caused by germs called bacteria. Back then, doctors hadn't yet discovered a cure, so Lien-teh had lain in bed for more than three weeks, exhausted and burning with fever, before he recovered. His mother and father wondered who would care for him if he got sick again.

But Lien-teh had worked too hard to miss this chance. And so, at the age of seventeen, he set out alone for the month-long journey, traveling by steamship to England, where he would study medicine at the University of Cambridge.

Once in college, Lien-teh flourished and won several awards,
including a scholarship to continue his research after graduation.

He plunged deeper into the study of germs, hoping to learn how to stop infections from spreading. Lien-teh traveled to institutes in England, France, and Germany and learned French and German while he probed bacteria and viruses that cause diseases such as malaria and tetanus.

After Lien-teh had finished his schooling, he was ready to go home. Late one night in early October 1903, his ship anchored off Penang, where friends and family had gathered to greet him and take him home. Reunited, Lien-teh and his parents wept at his safe return.

He hoped to join the government medical service in Malaya. But being of Chinese descent in a British colony, he faced discrimination. When he applied for a job, the authorities turned him away, saying it was open only to British citizens of European descent.

The rejection stung but didn't stop him. He spent a year studying at a new tropical-diseases institute in Kuala Lumpur, the capital city of Malaya. Afterward, he got married, started a family, and opened his own doctor's office in Penang. He cared for patients from early morning until late afternoon each day. A few years later, Lien-teh moved his family to China so he could help lead a new medical college there.

In December 1910, something happened that would change Lien-teh's life forever: a terrible disease swept into Northeast China. Local doctors didn't know why people were getting sick, and those who did get sick didn't survive. Because Lien-teh was famous for his expertise in germs, Chinese authorities asked him to travel north to Harbin, hoping he could save the city from this mysterious illness.

Even though he had to leave his family behind and put himself in danger, Lien-teh agreed to go because being a doctor meant helping people. His journey to Harbin, a city of Chinese and Russian people near the border with Russia, took three days by train. When he arrived on Christmas Eve, the temperature was –30°F (–35°C).

Doctors from Russia, France, and Japan had also come to Harbin to try to stop the outbreak. At first, doctors thought people were catching the disease from fleas or rats, as with earlier plagues. But when Lien-teh observed doctors getting sick soon after treating patients, he suspected that this disease spread some other way. He examined the body of a woman who had died from the disease and discovered the real culprit: a bacterial germ that spread when people coughed near each other.

He had to think of a way to stop these germs—and fast. Lunar New Year, the most important holiday in Chinese culture, was coming up in late January. If he didn't get the disease under control, it would spread even more quickly as families gathered to celebrate.

Just as he had done when he was school age, Lien-teh took what he had on hand and made something new. Using materials many people had in their homes, he created a new kind of mask to stop the germs, one that was sturdier than the masks he had seen doctors wear in Europe.

He used layers of gauze and cloth to create a thick mask that covered the entire face except for the eyes. The mask filtered germs out of the air to prevent the wearer from getting sick if someone coughed nearby. Doctors tied the layers tightly and securely so they wouldn't slip off, even in the harsh winter winds of Northeast China.

Lien-teh encouraged everyone to wear masks, but not all physicians in Harbin believed Lien-teh's mask would keep people safe. Some taunted him or called him a racist name. But the doctors who didn't wear masks got sick.

Soon, doctors at the plague hospital and citizens in the streets of Harbin were wearing masks. But Lien-teh's work wasn't done. He teamed up with Chinese and Russian authorities to quarantine the city. Russian leaders provided train cars to isolate those who had fallen ill, and Chinese soldiers prevented all residents from leaving and potentially spreading the disease to cities beyond Harbin.

By the time the Lunar New Year arrived, Lien-teh had the disease under better control. Deaths began to dwindle and hospital beds started to empty, and in March 1911, officials recorded the final case of the disease.

The plague was over. Lien-teh had stopped the spread in fewer than four months

His achievement stunned physicians and scientists worldwide. The following month, doctors and scientists from around the world converged at a conference in China to hear Lien-teh speak about his experience and how measures such as masks could help stop epidemics.

In 1918, when a flu virus was infecting people worldwide, many wore masks like the one Lien-teh had invented to slow the spread.

Long after the outbreak had ended, Lien-teh continued to try to keep people healthy, helping to establish hospitals and medical colleges throughout China that embraced medical advances as well as traditional healing. Because of his achievements, he was nominated for a Nobel Prize in 1935, the first person of Chinese descent to earn that honor.

Lien-teh's heroism kept a plague in China from ballooning into a worldwide crisis, likely saving millions of lives. More than one hundred years later, Lien-teh's innovations proved vital in the fight against COVID-19, when masks became part of everyday life.

When we wear a mask
to stop a disease,

we are all heroes—
just like Wu Lien-teh!

Time Line

March 10, 1879: *Born in Penang, Malaya (now Malaysia)*

1886: *Starts at Penang Free School*

1896: *Leaves for Cambridge University*

1902–1903: *Studies in England, Germany, and France*

1903: *Returns to Malaya to work for the Institute for Medical Research*

1908: *Moves to Tianjin, China*

December 24, 1910: *Arrives in Harbin to manage pneumonic plague*

March 1911: *Last recorded case of the pneumonic plague outbreak*

April 1911: *Chairs the International Plague Conference*

1912–1935: *Establishes fourteen hospitals and medical institutions in China*

1915–1920: *Cofounds the National Medical Association, later the Chinese Medical Association, and serves as secretary, then president*

1935: *Nominated for the Nobel Prize in Medicine*

1937: *Moves to Ipoh, Malaya, to practice medicine*

1960: *Dies, age eighty*

A Note from Dr. Shan Woo Liu

Wu Lien-teh was my great-grandfather. I grew up hearing stories about his work, and his autobiography, *Plague Fighter*, its worn cover depicting him with a microscope in hand, always sat on my family's coffee table. Since childhood, I dreamed of becoming a doctor and working in public health. Little did I know that a century after Wu Lien-teh confronted the pneumonic plague, I would be working on the front lines of the COVID-19 pandemic as an emergency physician. At the height of the pandemic, I was grateful for the mask he invented. His mask restricted entry and exit of particles and was an early version of the N95 mask, the mask that protected me and millions of others.

When schools shut down, I enrolled my first-grade daughter, Kaili, in an online writing class. One of Kaili's assignments was to write a nonfiction story. Given that mask recommendations emerged at that time, Kaili wrote her assignment on Wu Lien-teh, whom she had learned about two years earlier, when we traveled to Harbin, China, and visited the institute named for him.

As hate crimes against Asians grew over 2020 due to the pandemic, I noticed a lack of children's books featuring Asian heroes. *Masked Hero* emerged to share the history of how one man endured discrimination and doubt and invented a mask that helped end an epidemic. A portion of our proceeds from the sale of this book will be donated to organizations that work to improve racial equity and health care access.

To Learn More

Dr. Wu Lien-teh Society: https://wulientehsociety.org

Dr. Wu Lien-teh website: https://www.drwulienteh.com

Select Bibliography

"The Mask." *Throughline* podcast, May 14, 2020, 41:00. https://www.npr.org
/2020/05/13/855405132/the-mask.

Wilson, Mark. "The Untold Origin Story of the N95 Mask." *Fast Company*,
March 24, 2020. https://www.fastcompany.com/90479846/the-untold
-origin-story-of-the-n95-mask.

Wu Lien-teh. *Plague Fighter: The Autobiography of a Modern Chinese Physician.*
Cambridge, UK: W. Heffer and Sons, 1959.

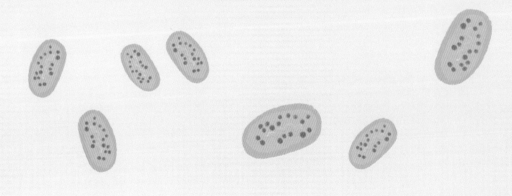

Shan Woo Liu is a great-granddaughter of Wu Lien-teh. She is an emergency medicine physician at Massachusetts General Hospital and an associate professor at Harvard Medical School. *Masked Hero* is her first picture book.

Lisa Wee is an illustrator who loves exploring the topics of diversity, cultural identity, and inclusivity with quaint and quirky characters. She is a Peranakan, with a blended cultural background of Chinese and Malay.

Acknowledgments

Thank you to my husband, Brian Gormley, for his love, patience, and careful edits. To Brooke Vitale and Kristin Zelazko for their fantastic wordsmithing. To Alec Shane of Writer's House for believing in this project and for his tremendous support. To MIT Kids Press and Candlewick for being pivotal in widely sharing this story. To Fae Kayarian for her enthusiasm and diligence. To Christina and Joe Morone, Marie Lee, Alison Chong, Yvonne Ho, and Julius Huang for their incredible advocacy and energy. To Tanya Paris for encouraging me to pursue this project and for inspiring Kaili to be a writer. To Ling Woo Liu for her love, insightful suggestions, and guidance. To my parents, Michael Wu Chunghao Liu and Catherine Huai-Sheng Liu, Kian Gormley, and Laura Liu for their steadfast love and support. To Lisa Wee for the beautiful illustrations. To Christos Lyteris, Lay Hong Ong, Wu Yu-lin, and Ailuen Wu's family for their help. And to Wu Lien-teh for his bravery.

First paperback edition 2024

Library of Congress Catalog Card Number 2022922830
ISBN 978-1-5362-2898-4 (hardcover)
ISBN 978-1-5362-3832-7 (paperback)

24 25 26 27 28 29 CCP 10 9 8 7 6 5 4 3 2 1

Printed in Shenzhen, Guangdong, China

This book was typeset in Bodoni Six.
The illustrations were created digitally.

MIT Kids Press
an imprint of Candlewick Press
99 Dover Street
Somerville, Massachusetts 02144

mitkidspress.com
candlewick.com